Practical
Chicken Dishes

p

This edition published by Parragon in 2007

Parragon
Queen Street House
4 Queen Street
Bath BA1 1HE, UK

ISBN: 978-1-4075-0249-6

Printed in China

NOTES FOR THE READER

Cup measurements in this book are for American cups.
This book also uses imperial and metric measurements. Follow the same units
of measurement throughout; do not mix imperial and metric.
All spoon measurements are level: teaspoons are assumed to be 5 ml, and
tablespoons are assumed to be 15 ml. Unless otherwise stated,
milk is assumed to be whole milk, eggs and individual vegetables such as potatoes
are medium, and pepper is freshly ground black pepper.

The nutritional information provided for each recipe is per serving or per person.
Optional ingredients, variations, or serving suggestions have
not been included in the calculations. The times given for each recipe are an approximate
guide only because the preparation times may differ according to the techniques used by
different people and the cooking times may vary as a result of the type of oven used.

Recipes using raw or very lightly cooked eggs should be
avoided by infants, the elderly, pregnant women, convalescents,
and anyone suffering from an illness.

Contents

Introduction

Chicken has become justly popular around the world and plays an important part in the modern diet, being reasonably priced and nutritionally sound. A versatile meat, it lends itself to an ample range of cooking methods and cuisines. Its unassertive flavor means that it is equally suited to cooking with sweet and savory flavors. Since it has a low fat content, especially without the skin, it is an ideal meat for low-cholesterol and calorie-controlled diets. An excellent source of protein, chicken contains valuable minerals, such as potassium and phosphorus, and some of the B vitamins.

Cooking methods for chicken

Roasting: remove any fat from the body cavity. Rinse the bird inside and out with water, then pat dry with paper towels. Season the cavity generously with salt and pepper, and add stuffing or herbs. Spread the breast with softened butter or oil. Set on a rack in a roasting pan or a shallow baking dish. Roast the bird, basting two or three times with the pan juices during roasting. If the chicken is browning too quickly, cover it with foil. Test that it is cooked (see Food safety and tips, opposite). Put the bird on a carving board and let rest for at least 15 minutes before serving. Make a sauce from the juices left in the roasting pan.

Broiling: a broiler's intense heat quickly seals the flesh beneath a crisp exterior. Place the chicken 4–6 inches/ 10–15 cm from a moderate heat source. If it browns too quickly, reduce the heat slightly. If the chicken is broiled too near the heat at too high a temperature, the outside will burn before the inside is cooked. If it is cooked for too long under low heat, it will dry out. Divide the chicken into joints to ensure even cooking. Breast meat, if cooked in one piece, can be dry, so it is best to cut it into chunks. Wings are best for fast broiling.

Deep-frying: this is suitable for small drumsticks, thighs, and joints. Dry the chicken pieces with paper towels to prevent spitting and so that they brown properly. The chicken may be coated in seasoned flour, egg, and bread crumbs, or a batter. Heat

a little oil or a mixture of oil and butter in a heavy skillet. When the oil is very hot, add the chicken pieces, skin-side down. Cook until golden brown all over, turning frequently. Drain well on paper towels before serving.

Sautéeing: this is ideal for small pieces or small birds, such as squabs. Heat a little oil or a mixture of oil and butter in a heavy skillet. Add the chicken and cook over a moderate heat until golden brown, turning frequently. Add bouillon or other liquid, bring to a boil, then cover and reduce the heat. Cook gently until cooked through.

Stir-frying: skinless, boneless chicken is cut into small pieces of equal size to ensure that the meat cooks evenly and stays succulent. Preheat a wok or a large skillet before adding a small amount of oil. When the oil starts to smoke, add the chicken and stir-fry with your chosen flavorings for 3–4 minutes, or until cooked through. Other ingredients can be cooked at the same time, or the chicken can be cooked by itself, then removed from the pan while you stir-fry the remaining ingredients. Return the chicken to the pan once the other ingredients are cooked.

Casseroling: this method is the best one for cooking joints from larger, more mature chickens, although smaller chickens can be cooked whole. The slow cooking produces tender meat with a good flavor. Brown the chicken in butter or oil or a mixture of both. Add

bouillon, wine, or a mixture of both, add seasonings and herbs, then cover and cook on top of the stove or in the oven until the chicken is tender. Add lightly sautéed vegetables about halfway through the cooking time.

Braising: this method does not involve adding liquid. Chicken pieces or a small whole chicken with vegetables are cooked at a low temperature in a preheated oven. Heat a little oil in an ovenproof and flameproof casserole, and gently cook the chicken until it is golden. Remove it and cook the vegetables until they are almost tender. Replace the chicken, cover tightly, and cook gently on the top of the stove or in an oven at a low temperature, until chicken and vegetables are tender.

Poaching: this gentle method produces tender chicken and a bouillon. Put a whole chicken, a bouquet garni, a leek, a carrot, and an onion in a large, flameproof casserole. Cover with water, season, and bring to a boil. Cover and simmer for 1½–2 hours, or until the chicken is tender. Lift it out, discard the bouquet garni, use the bouillon to make a sauce, and blend the vegetables to thicken the bouillon, or serve them with the chicken.

Food safety and tips

Chicken is liable to be contaminated by salmonella bacteria, which can cause severe food poisoning. When storing, handling, and preparing poultry, it is vital to observe the following precautions to prevent illness.
1. Check the "use by" date and the "best before" date. After buying, take the chicken home quickly, preferably in a freezer bag or a cooler box.
2. Place birds bought frozen in the freezer immediately.
3. To store in the refrigerator, remove wrappings and store giblets separately. Place the chicken in a shallow dish to catch drips. Cover loosely with foil and store on the bottom shelf for no more than two or three days, depending on the "best before" date. Avoid contact between raw chicken and cooked food during storage and preparation. Wash your hands thoroughly after handling raw chicken.
4. Prepare raw chicken on a cutting board that can be easily cleaned, such as a nonporous, plastic board.

5. Frozen birds should be defrosted before cooking. If time permits, defrost in the refrigerator for about 36 hours, or thaw for about 12 hours in a cool place. The flesh should feel soft and flexible, with no ice crystals. Bacteria breed in chicken thawing to room temperature. Cooking at high temperatures kills them, so cook the chicken as soon as possible after thawing.
6. Test that a chicken is cooked thoroughly by using a meat thermometer. The thigh should reach at least 175°F/79°C when cooked. Alternatively, pierce the thickest part of a thigh with a skewer, and the juices should run clear, not pink or red. Never partially cook chicken with the intention of completing cooking later.

Chicken bouillon

A well-flavored chicken bouillon is made from a whole bird, or the wings, carcass, and legs. A bouillon made from just chicken bones cooked with vegetables and flavorings will be less rich. A simple bouillon can be made from giblets (not the liver, which is bitter) with a bouquet garni, onion, carrot, and peppercorns. Homemade bouillon can be stored in the freezer for up to six months.

To make chicken bouillon, place a whole chicken, or wings and carcass, in a large pan with two onions cut into fourths. Cook until the chicken and onion are evenly browned. Cover with cold water, bring to a boil, and skim off any scum from the surface. Add two chopped carrots, two chopped celery stalks, a small bunch of parsley, a few bay leaves, a thyme sprig, and a few peppercorns. Partially cover and simmer for about 3 hours. Strain the bouillon into a bowl, let cool, then refrigerate. When it is cold, remove the fat that will have set on the surface.

KEY
Simplicity level 1–3 (1 easiest, 3 slightly harder)
Preparation time
Cooking time

Chicken & Bean Soup

This hearty and nourishing soup, combining garbanzo beans and chicken, is an ideal appetizer for a family supper, or it can make a snack on its own.

NUTRITIONAL INFORMATION

Calories	347	Sugars	.........2g
Protein	........28g	Fat	...........11g
Carbohydrate	...37g	Saturates	.......4g

15 mins   2 hrs 30 mins

SERVES 4

INGREDIENTS

2 tbsp butter

3 scallions, chopped

2 garlic cloves, crushed

sprig of fresh marjoram, finely chopped

12 oz/350 g boned chicken breasts, diced

5 cups chicken bouillon

12 oz/350 g canned garbanzo beans, drained

1 bouquet garni

1 red bell pepper, diced

1 green bell pepper, diced

4 oz/115 g small dried pasta shapes, such as elbow macaroni

salt and white pepper

croûtons, to serve

COOK'S TIP

If you prefer, you can use dried garbanzo beans. Cover with cold water and set aside to soak for 5–8 hours. Drain and add the beans to the soup, according to the recipe, and allow an additional 30 minutes–1 hour cooking time.

1 Melt the butter in a large pan. Add the scallions, garlic, sprig of fresh marjoram, and the diced chicken, and cook, stirring frequently, over medium heat for 5 minutes.

2 Add the chicken bouillon, garbanzo beans, and bouquet garni, then season with salt and white pepper.

3 Bring the soup to a boil, then lower the heat and simmer for about 2 hours.

4 Add the diced bell peppers and pasta shapes to the pan, then simmer for another 20 minutes.

5 Transfer the soup to a warm tureen. To serve, ladle the soup into individual serving bowls and serve immediately, garnished with the croûtons.

Chicken & Rice Soup

This soup is a good way of using up leftover cooked chicken and rice. Any type of rice is suitable, from white or brown long-grain rice to wild rice.

NUTRITIONAL INFORMATION

Calories ....165 Sugars 3g
Protein ....14g Fat 4g
Carbohydrate ...19g Saturates 1g

 10 mins   30 mins

SERVES 4

I N G R E D I E N T S

6⅓ cups chicken bouillon (see Cook's Tip, below)

2 small carrots, very thinly sliced

1 celery stalk, finely diced

1 baby leek, halved lengthwise and thinly sliced

4 oz/115 g tiny peas, defrosted if frozen

3 cups cooked rice

5½ oz/150 g cooked chicken, sliced

2 tsp chopped fresh tarragon

1 tbsp chopped fresh parsley

salt and pepper

fresh parsley sprigs, to garnish

1 Pour the bouillon into a large pan and add the carrots, celery, and leek. Bring to a boil, then reduce the heat to low and simmer the bouillon gently, partially covered, for 10 minutes.

2 Add the peas, rice, and chicken, and continue cooking for another 10–15 minutes, or until the vegetables are tender.

3 Add the chopped tarragon and parsley, then taste and adjust the seasoning, adding salt and pepper as needed.

4 Ladle the soup into warm bowls, garnish with parsley, and serve.

COOK'S TIP

If the bouillon you are using is a little on the weak side, or if you have used a bouillon cube, add the herbs at the beginning so that they can flavor the bouillon for a longer time.

Chicken & Asparagus Soup

This light, clear soup has a delicate flavor of asparagus and freshly picked herbs. Use a good quality bouillon for best results.

NUTRITIONAL INFORMATION

Calories	224	Sugars	.........2g
Protein	........27g	Fat	...........5g
Carbohydrate	...12g	Saturates	......1g

 5 mins   15 mins

SERVES 4

I N G R E D I E N T S

8 oz/225 g fresh asparagus

3½ cups fresh chicken bouillon (see page 5)

⅔ cup dry white wine

1 sprig each fresh parsley, dill, and tarragon

1 garlic clove

2¼ oz/60 g thin rice noodles

12 oz/350 g cooked lean chicken, finely shredded

salt and white pepper

1 small leek, to garnish

1 Wash the asparagus and trim away the woody ends. Cut each spear into pieces 1½ inches/4 cm long.

2 Pour the bouillon and wine into a large pan and bring to a boil.

3 Wash the herbs and tie them with clean string. Peel the garlic clove and add, with the herbs, to the pan together with the asparagus and noodles. Cover and simmer for 5 minutes.

4 Stir in the chicken and plenty of seasoning. Simmer gently for another 3-4 minutes, or until heated through.

5 Trim the leek, slice it down the center, then wash under running water to remove any dirt. Shake dry and shred finely.

6 Remove the herbs and garlic from the pan and discard. Ladle the soup into warm bowls, sprinkle with shredded leek, and serve at once.

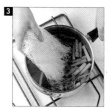

VARIATION

You can use any of your favorite herbs in this recipe, but choose those with a subtle flavor so that they do not overpower the asparagus. Small, tender asparagus spears give the best results and flavor.

Chicken & Leek Soup

This satisfying soup may be served as an entrée. Add rice and bell peppers to make it even more hearty and colorful.

NUTRITIONAL INFORMATION

Calories	183	Sugar	.........4g
Protein	........21g	Fats	...........9g
Carbohydrates	....4g	Saturates	......5g

 5 mins   1¼ hrs

SERVES 4–6

I N G R E D I E N T S

2 tbsp butter

12 oz/350 g leeks

12 oz/350 g boneless chicken

5 cups fresh chicken bouillon (see page 5)

1 bouquet garni

8 pitted prunes, halved

½ cup cooked rice and diced bell peppers, optional

salt and white pepper

1 Melt the butter in a large pan. Cut the leeks into 1-inch/2.5-cm pieces.

2 Add the chicken and leeks to the pan and cook for 8 minutes.

3 Next add the chicken bouillon and bouquet garni and stir together well.

4 Season the mixture well with salt and freshly ground pepper to taste.

5 Bring the soup to a boil and simmer for 45 minutes.

6 Add the pitted prunes to the pan, with the cooked rice and diced bell peppers if using, and simmer for about 20 minutes.

7 Remove the bouquet garni from the soup and discard. Serve the soup immediately.

VARIATION

Instead of the bouquet garni, you can use a bunch of fresh mixed herbs, tied together with string. Choose herbs such as parsley, thyme, and rosemary.

Chicken Pan Bagna

Perfect for a picnic, this Mediterranean-style sandwich can be prepared in very little time and in advance.

NUTRITIONAL INFORMATION

Calories ...... .366	Sugars 2g	
Protein .... .20g	Fat .... .23g	
Carbohydrate ...20g	Saturates 4g	

 5 mins   0 mins

SERVES 6

INGREDIENTS

1 large French stick

1 garlic clove

½ cup good-quality olive oil

¾ oz/20 g canned anchovy fillets

1¾ oz/50 g cold roast chicken

2 large tomatoes, sliced

8 large, pitted black olives, chopped

pepper

1 Using a sharp bread knife, cut the French stick in half lengthwise and open it out flat.

2 Cut the garlic clove in half and rub it liberally over the bread.

3 Lightly sprinkle the cut surface of the garlic-flavored bread with the olive oil, and let it soak in.

4 Drain the canned anchovies and set aside temporarily.

5 Thinly slice the chicken and arrange on top of the bread. Arrange the tomatoes and anchovies on top of the chicken.

6 Scatter over the olives and pepper. Sandwich the loaf back together and wrap in foil before serving in slices.

VARIATION

You could use Italian ciabatta or olive-studded focaccia instead of the French stick, if you prefer.

Spinach Salad

Fresh baby spinach is tasty and light, and it makes an excellent salad to go with the chicken and the creamy, orange-flavored dressing.

NUTRITIONAL INFORMATION

Calories	145	Sugars	.........3g
Protein	........10g	Fat	..........10g
Carbohydrate	....4g	Saturates	.......1g

 15 mins   0 mins

SERVES 4

I N G R E D I E N T S

1¾ oz/50 g mushrooms

3½ oz/100 g baby spinach, washed

2¾ oz/75 g radicchio, shredded

3½ oz/100 g cooked chicken breast

1¾ oz/50 g prosciutto

D R E S S I N G

2 tbsp olive oil

finely grated zest of ½ orange

juice of 1 orange

1 tbsp plain yogurt

1 Wipe the mushrooms with a damp cloth to remove any excess dirt.

2 Gently mix together the spinach and radicchio in a large bowl.

3 Using a sharp knife, thinly slice the wiped mushrooms and add them to the bowl containing the baby spinach and radicchio leaves, ready for the addition of the other salad ingredients.

4 Using your hands, tear the cooked chicken breast and prosciutto into strips and mix them thoroughly into the spinach salad.

5 To make the dressing, place the olive oil, orange zest, orange juice, and yogurt in a screw-top jar. Shake the jar until the mixture is well combined. Season to taste with salt and pepper.

6 Drizzle the dressing over the spinach salad and toss to mix well. Serve.

VARIATION

Spinach is delicious when served raw. Try raw spinach in a salad garnished with bacon or garlicky croûtons. The young leaves have a marvelously sharp flavor.

Chicken & Grape Salad

Tender chicken breast, sweet grapes, and crisp celery coated in a mild curry mayonnaise make a marvelous al fresco lunch.

NUTRITIONAL INFORMATION

Calories	413	Sugars	........20g
Protein	........39g	Fat	..........20g
Carbohydrate	...20g	Saturates	......3g

15 mins   0 mins

SERVES 4

INGREDIENTS

1 lb 2 oz/500 g cooked skinless, boneless chicken breasts

2 celery stalks, finely sliced

9 oz/250 g black grapes

generous ½ cup split almonds, toasted

pinch of paprika

sprigs of fresh cilantro or flatleaf parsley, to garnish

CURRY SAUCE

⅔ cup lowfat mayonnaise

4½ oz/125 g lowfat plain fromage frais or yogurt

1 tbsp clear honey

1 tbsp curry paste

1 Cut the chicken into fairly large pieces and transfer to a bowl with the sliced celery.

2 Halve the grapes, remove the seeds, and add to the bowl.

3 To make the curry sauce, mix together the mayonnaise, fromage frais, honey, and curry paste until blended.

4 Pour the curry sauce over the salad and then carefully mix together until thoroughly coated.

5 Transfer to serving plates and sprinkle over the split almonds and paprika.

6 Garnish the salad with sprigs of fresh cilantro or parsley.

COOK'S TIP
To save time, use seedless grapes, now widely available in supermarkets, and add them whole to the salad.

Old English Spicy Salad

This is an excellent recipe for using up leftover roast chicken. Add the dressing just before serving, so the spinach retains its crispness.

NUTRITIONAL INFORMATION

Calories 225	Sugars 4g	
Protein 25g	Fat 12g	
Carbohydrate 4g	Saturates 2g	

 10 mins   0 mins

SERVES 4

INGREDIENTS

8 oz/225 g young spinach leaves

3 celery stalks, thinly sliced

½ cucumber, thinly sliced

2 scallions, thinly sliced

3 tbsp chopped fresh parsley

12 oz/350g boneless, lean roast chicken, thinly sliced

smoked almonds, to garnish (optional)

DRESSING

1-inch/2.5-cm piece fresh gingerroot, finely grated

3 tbsp olive oil

1 tbsp white wine vinegar

1 tbsp clear honey

½ tsp ground cinnamon

salt and pepper

1 Thoroughly wash and dry the young spinach leaves.

2 Toss the celery, cucumber, and scallions with the spinach and parsley in a large bowl.

3 Transfer the salad ingredients to serving plates and arrange the chicken over the salad.

4 To make the dressing, combine the grated ginger, olive oil, wine vinegar, honey, and cinnamon in a screw-topped jar and shake well to mix. Season with salt and pepper to taste.

5 Pour the dressing over the salad. Scatter a few smoked almonds over the salad to garnish, if using.

COOK'S TIP

For extra color, add some cherry tomatoes and thin strips of red and yellow bell peppers, and garnish with a little grated carrot.

Lemongrass Skewers

An unusual recipe in which fresh lemongrass stems are used as skewers. The lemongrass imparts its delicate lemon flavor to the chicken mixture.

NUTRITIONAL INFORMATION

Calories 140   Sugars 2g
Protein . . . . .19g   Fat 7g
Carbohydrate . . . .2g   Saturates 1g

10 mins   20 mins

SERVES 4

INGREDIENTS

2 long or 4 short lemongrass stems

2 large, boneless, skinless chicken breasts (about 14 oz/400 g), roughly chopped

1 small egg white

1 carrot, finely grated

1 small red chile, seeded and chopped

2 tbsp fresh garlic chives, chopped

2 tbsp fresh cilantro, chopped

1 tbsp sunflower oil

salt and pepper

cilantro and lime slices, to garnish

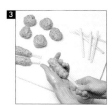

1 If the lemongrass stems are long, cut them in half across the middle to make 4 short lengths. Cut each stem in half lengthwise, so you have 8 lemongrass stems altogether.

COOK'S TIP

If you can't find whole lemongrass stems, use wooden or bamboo skewers instead, and add ½ teaspoon ground lemongrass to the mixture with the other flavorings.

2 Place the the chicken pieces in a food processor with the egg white. Process to a smooth paste, then add the carrot, chile, chives, cilantro, and salt and pepper. Process for a few seconds to mix well.

3 Chill the mixture in the refrigerator for about 15 minutes. Divide the mixture into 8 equal portions, and use your hands to shape the mixture around the lemongrass skewers.

4 Brush the skewers with oil, then cook under a preheated medium-hot broiler for 4–6 minutes, turning them occasionally, until golden brown and thoroughly cooked. Alternatively, grill over medium-hot coals.

5 Serve hot, garnished with slices of lime and cilantro.

Sticky Ginger Chicken Wings

A finger-licking appetizer of chicken wings or drumsticks, which is ideal for parties (have finger bowls ready).

NUTRITIONAL INFORMATION

Calories	416	Sugars	.........5g
Protein	........41g	Fat	.........25g
Carbohydrate	....7g	Saturates	.......7g

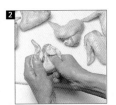

15 mins, plus several hrs for marinating

15 mins

SERVES 4

INGREDIENTS

2 garlic cloves, peeled

1 piece preserved ginger in syrup

1 tsp coriander seeds

2 tbsp preserved ginger syrup

2 tbsp dark soy sauce

1 tbsp lime juice

1 tsp sesame oil

12 chicken wings

lime wedges and fresh cilantro leaves,
  to garnish

1 Roughly chop the garlic and ginger. In a pestle and mortar, crush the garlic, preserved ginger, and coriander seeds to a paste, gradually working in the ginger syrup, soy sauce, lime juice, and sesame oil.

2 Tuck the pointed tip of each chicken wing underneath the thicker end of the wing to make a neat triangular shape. Place in a large bowl.

3 Add the garlic and ginger paste to the bowl and toss the chicken wings in the mixture to coat evenly. Cover and let marinate in the refrigerator for several hours, or overnight.

4 Arrange the chicken wings in one layer on a foil-lined broiler pan and cook under a preheated medium-hot broiler for 12–15 minutes, turning them occasionally, until golden brown and thoroughly cooked. Alternatively, cook on a lightly oiled barbecue grill over medium-hot coals for 12–15 minutes. Serve garnished with lime wedges and fresh cilantro.

COOK'S TIP

To test if the chicken is cooked, pierce it deeply through the thickest part of the flesh. When fully cooked, the chicken juices are clear, with no trace of pink. If there is any trace of pink, cook for a few more minutes.

Chicken & Mango Stir-Fry

A colorful, exotic mix of flavors that works surprisingly well in a dish that is easy and quick to cook—ideal for a midweek family meal.

NUTRITIONAL INFORMATION

Calories 200	Sugars 5g
Protein 23g	Fat 6g
Carbohydrate 7g	Saturates 1g

15 mins   12 mins

SERVES 4

I N G R E D I E N T S

6 boneless, skinless chicken thighs

2 tsp grated fresh gingerroot

1 garlic clove, crushed

1 small red chile, seeded

1 large red bell pepper

4 scallions

7 oz/200 g snow peas

3½ oz/100 g baby corn cobs

1 large, firm, ripe mango

2 tbsp sunflower oil

1 tbsp light soy sauce

3 tbsp rice wine or sherry

1 tsp sesame oil

salt and pepper

snipped chives, to garnish

1 Cut the chicken into long, thin strips and place in a bowl. Mix together the ginger, garlic, and chile, then stir into the chicken strips to coat them evenly.

2 Thinly slice the bell pepper, cutting diagonally. Trim and diagonally slice the scallions. Cut the snow peas and corn cobs in half diagonally. Peel the mango, remove the pit, and slice thinly.

3 Heat the oil in a wok or large skillet over high heat. Add the chicken and stir-fry for 4–5 minutes, or until just turning golden brown. Add the bell peppers and stir-fry over medium heat for 4–5 minutes to soften them.

4 Add the scallions and snow peas together with the corn cobs and stir-fry for another minute.

5 In a separate bowl, mix together the soy sauce, rice wine or sherry, and sesame oil and stir the mixture into the wok with the rest of the ingredients. Add the mango and stir gently for 1 minute to heat thoroughly.

6 Adjust the seasoning with salt and pepper to taste and serve immediately garnished with snipped chives.

Green Chicken Curry

Thai curries are traditionally very hot, and they make a little go a long way. The spiced juices are eaten with rice to "stretch" a small amount of meat.

NUTRITIONAL INFORMATION

Calories	193	Sugars	.........9g
Protein	........22g	Fat	..........8g
Carbohydrate	....9g	Saturates	.......1g

 5 mins 45 mins

SERVES 4

INGREDIENTS

6 boneless, skinless chicken thighs

1¾ cups coconut milk

2 garlic cloves, crushed

2 tbsp Thai fish sauce

2 tbsp Thai green curry paste

12 baby eggplants (or Thai pea eggplants)

3 green chiles, finely chopped

3 kaffir lime leaves, shredded

4 tbsp chopped fresh cilantro

salt and pepper

boiled rice, to serve

1 Cut the chicken into bite-size pieces. Pour the coconut milk into a wok or large skillet over high heat and bring to a boil.

2 Add the garlic, fish sauce, and chicken to the pan and bring back to a boil. Lower the heat and simmer gently for 30 minutes, or until the chicken is tender.

3 Remove the chicken from the mixture with a perforated spoon. Set aside and keep warm.

4 Stir the green curry paste into the pan with the eggplants, chiles, and lime leaves, and simmer for 5 minutes.

5 Return the chicken to the pan and bring to a boil. Adjust the seasoning to taste with salt and pepper, then stir in the cilantro. Serve with boiled rice.

COOK'S TIP

Baby eggplants, or "pea eggplants" as they are called in Thailand, are traditionally used, but not always available outside the country. If you cannot find them in an Asian food store, use chopped ordinary eggplant or a few green peas.

Harlequin Chicken

This colorful dish will tempt the appetites of all the family. Infants enjoy the fun shapes of the multicolored bell peppers.

NUTRITIONAL INFORMATION

Calories 183	Sugar 8g	
Protein 24g	Fats 6g	
Carbohydrates 8g	Saturates 1g	

5 mins   25 mins

SERVES 4

INGREDIENTS

10 skinless, boneless chicken thighs

1 onion

1 each red, green, and yellow bell peppers

1 tbsp sunflower oil

14 oz/400 g canned chopped tomatoes

2 tbsp chopped fresh parsley

pepper

whole-wheat bread and salad, to serve

1 Using a sharp knife, cut the chicken thighs into bite-size pieces.

2 Peel and thinly slice the onion. Halve and seed the bell peppers and cut into small diamond shapes.

3 Heat the sunflower oil in a shallow pan, then quickly cook the chicken and onion until golden.

4 Add the peppers and cook for 2–3 minutes, then stir in the canned tomatoes and chopped fresh parsley, and season with pepper.

5 Cover the pan tightly and simmer for approximately 15 minutes, or until the chicken and vegetables are tender. Remove from the pan and serve hot with whole-wheat bread and salad greens.

COOK'S TIP

If you're making this dish for small children, the chicken can be finely chopped or ground first.

Squabs in Green Marinade

Marinated before cooking in a green herb mixture, these elegant squabs are packed with lively Mexican flavors.

NUTRITIONAL INFORMATION

Calories	614	Sugars	. . . . .6g
Protein	. . . . .44g	Fat	. . . . .49g
Carbohydrate	. . . .8g	Saturates	. . . . . .19g

10 mins, plus at least 3 hrs marinating

45 mins

SERVES 4

I N G R E D I E N T S

10 garlic cloves, chopped

juice of 1 lime

1 bunch fresh cilantro, finely chopped

½ fresh green chile, seeded and chopped

1 tsp ground cumin

4 squabs

12 oz/350 g plain yogurt

1 red bell pepper, roasted, skinned, seeded, and diced

¼–1 tsp marinade from chipotle canned in adobo, or chipotle salsa

3–5 scallions, thinly sliced

handful of toasted pumpkin seeds

salt and pepper

1 In a bowl, combine 9 garlic cloves with the lime juice, three-fourths of the cilantro, the green chile, and half the cumin. Press the mixture onto the squabs and marinate for at least 3 hours in the refrigerator, or preferably overnight.

2 Place the squabs in a roasting pan and cook in a preheated oven at 400°F/200°C for 15 minutes. To check whether it is cooked, pierce the thigh with a knife. If the juices run clear, the squab is cooked; if necessary, return to the oven and continue to roast.

3 Meanwhile, mix the plain yogurt with the bell pepper, chipotle marinade, and the remaining garlic and cumin. Season with salt and pepper to taste.

4 Serve each squab individually with a spoonful of the bell pepper sauce and a sprinkling of the remaining fresh cilantro, the scallions, and the pumpkin seeds. Serve the dish at once while the chicken is still piping hot.

VARIATION

For grilled lamb, skewer lamb chunks, such as shoulder or leg, onto metal or soaked bamboo skewers. Marinate in the green herbed marinade as in step 1, then cook over hot coals.

Potato, Leek & Chicken Pie

This pie has an attractive phyllo shell with a ruffled top made from strips of the dough brushed with melted butter.

NUTRITIONAL INFORMATION

Calories	543	Sugars 7g
Protein	........21g	Fat 27g
Carbohydrate	...56g	Saturates 16g

15 mins   1 hr 5 mins

SERVES 4

INGREDIENTS

8 oz/225 g waxy potatoes, cubed

5 tbsp butter

1 skinned chicken breast fillet (about
  6 oz/175 g), cubed

1 leek, sliced

5½ oz/150 g chestnut mushrooms, sliced

2½ tbsp all-purpose flour

1¼ cups milk

1 tbsp Dijon mustard

2 tbsp chopped fresh sage

8 oz/225 g phyllo pastry, thawed if frozen

3 tbsp butter, melted

salt and pepper

1 Cook the cubed potatoes in a pan of boiling water for 5 minutes then drain.

2 Melt the butter in a skillet and cook the chicken cubes for 5 minutes.

3 Add the leek and mushrooms, and cook for 3 minutes, stirring. Stir in the flour and cook for 1 minute. Gradually add the milk and bring to a boil. Add the mustard, sage, and potatoes, season, then simmer for 10 minutes.

4 Meanwhile, line a deep pie dish with half the sheets of phyllo. Spoon the sauce into the dish and cover with one

sheet of phyllo. Brush the phyllo with melted butter and lay another sheet on top. Brush this sheet with more butter.

5 Cut the remaining phyllo into strips and fold them on top of the pie creating a ruffled effect. Brush with melted butter and cook in a preheated oven, 350°F/180°C, for 45 minutes, or until golden brown and crisp. Serve hot.

COOK'S TIP

If the top of the pie starts to brown too quickly, cover it with foil halfway through the cooking time to let the bottom cook through without the top burning.

Chicken with Orange Sauce

The refreshing combination of chicken and orange sauce with whole-wheat spaghetti makes this a perfect dish for a warm summer evening.

NUTRITIONAL INFORMATION

Calories ....933 Sugars 34g
Protein ....74g Fat 24g
Carbohydrate ..100g Saturates 5g

 10 mins   35 mins

SERVES 4

INGREDIENTS

2 tbsp rapeseed oil

3 tbsp olive oil

4 chicken suprêmes, about 8 oz/225 g each

⅔ cup orange brandy

2 tbsp all-purpose flour

⅔ cup freshly squeezed orange juice

1 oz/25 g zucchini, cut into matchstick strips

1 oz/25 g red bell pepper, cut into matchstick strips

1 oz/25 g leek, finely shredded

14 oz/400 g dried whole-wheat spaghetti

3 large oranges, peeled and cut into segments

zest of 1 orange, cut into very fine strips

2 tbsp chopped fresh tarragon

⅔ cup ricotta cheese

salt and pepper

fresh tarragon leaves, to garnish

1 Heat the rapeseed oil and 1 tbsp of the olive oil in a skillet. Add the chicken and cook quickly, until golden brown. Add the orange brandy and cook for 3 minutes. Sprinkle over the flour and cook for 2 minutes.

2 Lower the heat and add the orange juice, zucchini, bell pepper, and leek, and season to taste. Simmer for 5 minutes, or until the sauce has thickened.

3 Meanwhile, bring a pan of salted water to a boil. Add the spaghetti and 1 tbsp of the olive oil and cook for 10 minutes. Drain, then transfer to a serving dish and drizzle over the remaining oil.

4 Add half the orange segments, half the orange zest, the tarragon, and ricotta cheese to the sauce in the pan and cook for 3 minutes.

5 Place the chicken on top of the spaghetti, pour over a little sauce, garnish with the remaining orange segments and zest. Garnish with fresh tarragon leaves and serve immediately.

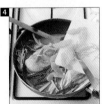

Prosciutto-Wrapped Chicken

Stuffed with ricotta, nutmeg, and spinach, and wrapped in wafer-thin slices of prosciutto, this chicken is then gently cooked in white wine.

NUTRITIONAL INFORMATION

Calories 426   Sugars 4g
Protein . . . . .44g   Fat 21g
Carbohydrate . . . .9g   Saturates 8g

20 mins   40 mins

SERVES 4

I N G R E D I E N T S

4¼ oz/125 g frozen spinach, defrosted

generous ½ cup ricotta cheese

pinch of grated nutmeg

4 skinless, boneless chicken breasts (each weighing about 6 oz/175 g)

4 slices prosciutto

2 tbsp butter

1 tbsp olive oil

12 small onions or shallots

4½ oz/125 g button mushrooms, sliced

1 tbsp all-purpose flour

⅔ cup dry white or red wine

1¼ cups chicken bouillon

salt and pepper

carrot puree and green beans, to serve

1 Put the spinach into a strainer and press out the water with a spoon. Mix with the ricotta and nutmeg, then season with salt and pepper to taste.

2 Using a sharp knife, slit each chicken breast through the side and enlarge each cut to form a pocket. Fill each cut with the spinach mixture, then reshape the chicken breasts to enclose the mixture. Wrap each breast tightly in a slice of prosciutto, and secure with toothpicks. Cover and chill in the refrigerator.

3 Heat the butter and oil in a skillet and brown the chicken breasts for at least 2 minutes on each side. Lift out and transfer the chicken to a large, shallow, ovenproof dish. Keep warm until required.

4 Put the onions and mushrooms in the skillet and cook for 2–3 minutes, or until lightly browned. Stir in the all-purpose flour, then gradually add the wine and bouillon. Bring to a boil, stirring constantly. Season to taste, and spoon the mixture around the chicken.

5 Cook the chicken, uncovered, in a preheated oven, 400°F/200°C, for 20 minutes. Turn the breasts over and cook for another 10 minutes. Remove the toothpicks and serve with the sauce, together with carrot puree and green beans.

Chicken Risotto Milanese

This simple chicken risotto is one of Italy's best-known dishes, served in restaurants all over the world. But every cook varies the recipe slightly.

NUTRITIONAL INFORMATION	
Calories 857	Sugars 1g
Protein 57g	Fat 38g
Carbohydrate ...72g	Saturates 21g

5 mins

1 hr 5 mins

SERVES 4

INGREDIENTS

generous ½ cup butter

2 lb/900 g chicken, thinly sliced

1 large onion, chopped

1 lb 2 oz/500 g risotto rice

2½ cups chicken bouillon

⅔ cup white wine

1 tsp crumbled saffron

salt and pepper

generous ½ cup grated Parmesan cheese, to serve

1 Heat 4 tbsp of butter in a deep skillet, and cook the chicken and onion until golden brown.

2 Add the rice to the skillet, stir well, then cook for 15 minutes.

3 Heat the bouillon until boiling and gradually stir it into the rice. Add the white wine, saffron, salt and pepper, and mix well. Simmer gently for 20 minutes, stirring occasionally, and adding more bouillon if the risotto becomes too dry.

4 Let the risotto stand for 2–3 minutes then, just before serving, add a little more bouillon and simmer for 10 minutes. Divide the risotto between individual plates and serve sprinkled with grated Parmesan and the remaining butter.

Lemon Chicken

This is on everyone's list of favorite Chinese dishes, perhaps because it is so simple to make. Serve with stir-fried vegetables for a delicious meal.

NUTRITIONAL INFORMATION

Calories . . . . . . .272 Sugars 1g
Protein . . . . . . .36g Fat 11g
Carbohydrate . . . .5g Saturates 2g

 5 mins   15 mins

SERVES 4

I N G R E D I E N T S

vegetable oil, for deep-frying

1 lb 7 oz/650 g skinless, boneless chicken, cut into strips

S A U C E

1 tbsp cornstarch

6 tbsp cold water

3 tbsp fresh lemon juice

2 tbsp sweet sherry

½ tsp superfine sugar

T O   G A R N I S H

lemon slices

shredded scallion

1 Heat the oil for deep-frying in a wok or skillet to 350°F/180°C, or until a bread cube browns in 30 seconds.

2 Lower the heat and cook the chicken strips for 3–4 minutes, or until cooked through.

3 Remove the chicken with a slotted spoon, set aside, and keep warm. Drain the oil from the wok.

4 To make the sauce, in a pitcher mix the cornstarch with 2 tablespoons of the water to form a paste.

5 Pour the lemon juice and the remaining water into the wok.

6 Add the sherry and superfine sugar and bring to a boil, stirring until the sugar has completely dissolved.

7 Stir in the cornstarch paste and return to a boil. Lower the heat and simmer, stirring constantly, for 2–3 minutes, or until the sauce is thickened and clear.

8 Transfer the chicken to a warm serving plate and pour the sauce over the top. Garnish with the lemon slices and shredded scallion and serve immediately.

COOK'S TIP

If you would prefer to use chicken portions rather than strips, cook them in the oil, covered, over low heat for about 30 minutes, or until cooked through.

Peanut Sesame Chicken

Sesame seeds and peanuts give extra crunch and flavor to this stir-fry, and the fruit juice glaze gives the sauce a glossy coating.

NUTRITIONAL INFORMATION

Calories ....435 Sugars 10g
Protein ....38g Fat 26g
Carbohydrate ...14g Saturates 4g

10 mins   15 mins

SERVES 4

INGREDIENTS

2 tbsp vegetable oil

2 tbsp sesame oil

1 lb 2 oz/500 g boneless, skinless chicken breasts, sliced into strips

9 oz/250 g broccoli, divided into small florets

9 oz/250 g baby or dwarf corn, halved if large

1 small, red bell pepper, seeded and sliced

2 tbsp soy sauce

1 cup orange juice

2 tsp cornstarch

2 tbsp sesame seeds, toasted

2¼ oz/60 g shelled unsalted peanuts, roasted

rice or noodles, to serve

1 Heat the oils in a large, heavy-bottomed skillet or wok until smoking. Add the chicken strips and stir-fry for about 4–5 minutes, or until browned.

2 Add the broccoli, corn, and red bell pepper, and stir-fry over high heat for 1–2 minutes, until they just soften.

3 Meanwhile, in a bowl, mix the soy sauce together with the orange juice and the cornstarch. Pour into the chicken and vegetable mixture, stirring constantly, until the sauce has thickened slightly and a glaze develops.

4 Stir in the sesame seeds and peanuts, mixing well. Continue to stir-fry for another 3–4 minutes.

5 Transfer the stir-fry to a warm serving dish and serve with rice or noodles.

COOK'S TIP

Make sure you use the unsalted variety of peanuts or the dish will be too salty, because the soy sauce adds extra saltiness.

Chicken & Rice Casserole

This is a quick-cooking, spicy casserole of rice, chicken, and vegetables in an aromatic soy and ginger-flavored liquor.

NUTRITIONAL INFORMATION

Calories	502	Sugars	........2g
Protein	........55g	Fat	..........9g
Carbohydrate	...52g	Saturates	.......3g

🍲 15 mins, plus 30 mins marinating   ⏰ 45 mins

SERVES 4

INGREDIENTS

1½ cups long-grain rice

1 tbsp dry sherry

2 tbsp light soy sauce

2 tbsp dark soy sauce

2 tsp dark brown sugar

1 tsp salt

1 tsp sesame oil

900 g/2 lb skinless, boneless chicken meat, diced

3½ cups chicken bouillon

2 open cup mushrooms, sliced

60 g/2¼ oz water chestnuts, halved

75 g/2¾ oz broccoli florets

1 yellow bell pepper, sliced

4 tsp grated fresh gingerroot

whole chives, to garnish

1 In a bowl, mix together the sherry, soy sauces, sugar, salt, and sesame oil.

2 Stir the chicken into the soy mixture, turning to coat the chicken well. Let marinate for about 30 minutes.

3 Cook the rice in boiling water for 15 minutes. Drain well, rinse under cold water, then drain again thoroughly.

4 Bring the bouillon to a boil in a large pan or wok. Add the chicken with the marinade, mushrooms, water chestnuts, broccoli, bell pepper, and ginger.

5 Stir in the rice, reduce the heat, then cover and cook for 25-30 minutes, or until the chicken and vegetables are cooked through. Transfer to serving plates, garnish with chives, and serve.

VARIATION

This dish would work equally well with beef or pork. Chinese dried mushrooms may be used instead of the open-cup mushrooms, if rehydrated before adding to the dish.

Braised Chicken

A glaze served as a sauce with the chicken gives this straightforward dish a professional touch.

NUTRITIONAL INFORMATION

Calories	294	Sugars 9g
Protein	........31g	Fat 15g
Carbohydrate	...10g	Saturates 3g

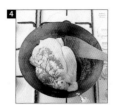

10 mins

1 hr 15 mins

SERVES 4

I N G R E D I E N T S

1 whole chicken, about 3 lb 5 oz/1.5 kg

3 tbsp vegetable oil

1 tbsp peanut oil

2 tbsp dark brown sugar

5 tbsp dark soy sauce

⅔ cup water

2 garlic cloves, crushed

1 small onion, chopped

1 fresh red chile, chopped

celery leaves and whole chives, to garnish

1 Preheat a large wok or large skillet in preparation.

2 Clean the chicken inside and out with damp paper towels.

3 Place the vegetable oil and peanut oil in the wok, then add the dark brown sugar and heat together gently until the sugar caramelizes.

4 Stir the soy sauce into the wok. Add the chicken and turn it in the mixture to coat thoroughly on all sides.

5 Add the water, crushed garlic, chopped onion, and chopped chile. Cover the pan and simmer, turning the chicken occasionally, for about 1 hour, or until cooked through.

6 Remove the chicken from the wok and set it to one side. Increase the heat and reduce the sauce in the wok until it has thickened. Transfer the chicken to a serving plate. Garnish with celery leaves and whole chives, and serve with the sauce.

COOK'S TIP
For a spicier sauce, add 1 tbsp of finely chopped fresh ginger and 1 tbsp ground Szechuan peppercorns with the chile in step 5.

Chicken with a Yogurt Crust

A spicy, Indian-style coating is baked around lean chicken to give a full flavor. Serve with a tomato, cucumber, and cilantro relish.

NUTRITIONAL INFORMATION

Calories	176	Sugars	........5g
Protein	........30g	Fat	..........4g
Carbohydrate	....5g	Saturates	......1g

🍙 🍙

🍧 10 mins   🕐 35 mins

SERVES 4

INGREDIENTS

1 garlic clove, crushed

1-inch/2.5-cm piece fresh gingerroot, finely chopped

1 fresh green chile, seeded and finely chopped

6 tbsp lowfat plain yogurt

1 tbsp tomato paste

1 tsp ground turmeric

1 tsp garam masala

1 tbsp lime juice

4 boneless, skinless chicken breasts (4¼ oz/125 g each)

salt and pepper

wedges of lime or lemon, to serve

RELISH

4 tomatoes

¼ cucumber

1 small red onion

2 tbsp chopped fresh cilantro

1 Preheat the oven to 375°F/190°C and have ready a mixing bowl and a cookie sheet.

2 Place the garlic, ginger, chile, yogurt, tomato paste, spices, lime juice, and seasoning in a bowl and mix to combine all the ingredients.

3 Wash and pat dry the chicken breasts thoroughly with absorbent paper towels and then place them on the cookie sheet.

4 Spread the spicy yogurt mixture over the chicken and bake in the preheated oven for 30–35 minutes, or until the meat is tender and cooked through.

5 Meanwhile, make the relish. Finely chop the tomatoes, cucumber, and onion, and mix in a bowl with the cilantro. Season with salt and pepper to taste, then cover and chill in the refrigerator until required.

6 Drain the cooked chicken on absorbent paper towels and serve hot with the relish and wedges of lime or lemon. Alternatively, let cool, then chill for at least 1 hour and serve sliced as part of a salad.